Let Us Remember

A Resource Book of
Communion Meditations

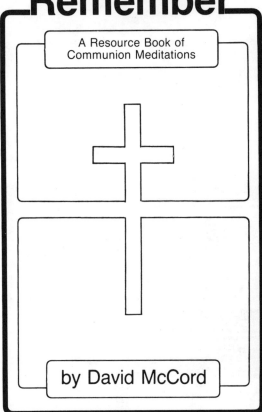

by David McCord

STANDARD PUBLISHING

Cincinnati, Ohio   3023

Scripture quotations are from the *Revised Standard Version* of the Bible.

Library of Congress Cataloging in Publication Data

McCord, David M.
  Let us remember.

  1. Lord's Supper—Meditations. I. Title.
  BV826.5.M4   1986   264'.36   86-3743
  ISBN 0-87403-071-4

WG.04

Contents

Preface

It was in the breaking of bread that the two disciples from Emmaus were awakened as to the identity of the risen Lord. Today this same kind of experience is reenacted every Lord's Day. Christians around the world break bread together and see in the broken bread, His body, and in the cup, His blood. In the act of Communion we see Jesus, our crucified and risen Lord.

This memorial meal has been ordained by our Lord. We are to observe it faithfully in remembrance of Him. Just as the cross is central to the gospel, so the Lord's Supper is central to the worship of the church. The purpose for having a meditation is to help the worshiper prepare to partake of the loaf and the cup in a worthy manner, with reverence and understanding.

The meditations and resources in this book will help accomplish that purpose. Please feel free to use them as they are written or change and adapt them to your own or to your congregation's needs.

Communion Meditations for Every Lord's Day

Acceptance

The Lord's Supper reminds us that we have accepted, and that we continue to accept, Jesus Christ into our lives. "He came to his own home, and his own people received him not. But to all who received him, who believed in his name, he gave power to become children of God" (John 1:11, 12).

You are children of God! That is possible because He first loved and accepted you, and now you have accepted His Son Jesus into your life.

You first established this relationship as God's child when you put your faith in Jesus as the Son of God and were baptized into Him. You maintain this relationship as you imitate Christ in your daily life.

As you accept and partake of these emblems, remember that you have accepted Jesus and that He has accepted you. Use this time to rededicate yourself to this continuing relationship.

Date Used: _____

Assurance

We have confidence in God, and we know that we are ransomed from sin and death, because of Jesus' death on the cross.

"You know that you were ransomed from the futile ways inherited from your fathers, not with perishable things such as silver or gold, but with the precious blood of Christ, like that of a lamb without blemish or spot. . . . Through him you have confidence in God" (1 Peter 1:18, 19, 21a).

The apostle John stated this idea in slightly different terms, but with equal certainty.

"He who has the Son has life; he who has not the Son of God has not life. I write this to you who believe in the name of the Son of God, that you may know that you have eternal life" (1 John 5:12, 13).

We come to this table in confidence with this assurance. Jesus died on the cross to forgive us of our sins; in Him we know we have life, both now and forever!

Date Used: _____

Atonement

The Lord's Supper is filled with rich meaning, yet it is often taken for granted or misunderstood.

When the parents of a seven-year-old boy were to be baptized one Sunday, they took their son into the service with them. They had explained to him about baptism, but they failed to say anything about the Communion.

After church they asked him what he thought about everything. "Well," he complained, "those little cookies really weren't very good, and then they didn't give you enough Kool-aid to wash them down."

Paul presents a mature understanding of Christ's atoning death in Colossians 1:21, 22. "And you, who once were estranged and hostile in mind, doing evil deeds, he has now reconciled in his body of flesh by his death, in order to present you holy and blameless and irreproachable before him."

In these emblems we see the broken body and shed blood of our crucified Lord. And we are reminded that by His death we are forgiven of our sins and reconciled to our God.

Date Used: _____

Blood

A missionary to Africa told how a man was bitten on the foot by a deadly puff adder snake. He was brought to a clinic where an anti-venom serum was administered, which saved the man's life.

Before he was brought to the clinic, however, a local custom was carried out. A goat was slaughtered and its blood poured on the man's head and all over his body. It was thought that the blood might somehow purify his body of the poison and save his life.

The Jews used the blood of animals, according to God's dictate, for outward purification. But the inward problem of sin still remained.

The blood of Jesus contains no literal or medicinal properties. But the shedding of His blood represents the giving of His life, the one sacrifice that God accepts for our forgiveness and spiritual cleansing.

"For if the sprinkling of defiled persons with the

9

blood of goats and bulls and with the ashes of a heifer sanctifies for the purification of the flesh, how much more shall the blood of Christ, who through the eternal Spirit offered himself without blemish to God, purify your conscience from dead works to serve the living God" (Hebrews 9:13, 14).

Date Used: _____ _____

Bread of Life

"I am the bread of life," Jesus said. "Your fathers ate the manna in the wilderness, and they died. This is the bread which comes down from heaven, that a man may eat of it and not die. I am the living bread which came down from heaven; if any one eats of this bread, he will live for ever; and the bread which I shall give for the life of the world is my flesh" (John 6:48-51).

Must we literally eat the flesh of Jesus and drink His blood? Is that what this Communion service is all about? Of course not.

Jesus went on to explain, "Do you take offense at this? Then what if you were to see the Son of man ascending where he was before? It is the spirit that gives life, the flesh is of no avail; the words that I have spoken to you are spirit and life" (John 6:61b-63).

We cannot eat His flesh and drink His blood because they are not available to us. He has ascended on high and is with the Father.

What is it then that we are to consume? His words (v. 63). As we receive Jesus into our lives and live daily by His teachings and according to His words, we have life in us. "The words that I have spoken to you are spirit and life."

These emblems are reminders that Jesus abides in us and that we are committed to consuming His word and to living by His teachings.

Date Used: _____

Brotherhood

In THE BIG FISHERMAN by Lloyd C. Douglas, Voldi describes Jesus this way—"The man has a compelling voice. I can't describe it or the effect of it. It's a unifying voice that converts a great crowd of mutually distrustful strangers into a tight little group of blood brothers."

That is what we are! Blood brothers! But it is not merely Christ's compelling voice or His winsome ways that does this. Through His death on the cross and by the shedding of His blood we are made one in Him.

"The cup of blessing which we bless, is it not a participation in the blood of Christ? The bread which we break, is it not a participation in the body of Christ? Because there is one bread, we who are many are one body, for we all partake of the one bread" (1 Corinthians 10:16, 17).

Because we are in Communion with Christ, we have Communion with one another. We have many differences, but this one thing we have in common: Jesus Christ is our Lord and Savior. Because of Him we belong to each other. We are blood brothers.

Date Used: _____

Confession

The following bit of graffiti was found on a wall at St. John's University.

"Jesus said unto them, 'Who do you say that I am?'

"And they replied, 'You are the eschatological manifestation of the ground of our being, the kerygma in which we find the ultimate meaning of our interpersonal relationships.'

"And Jesus said, 'What?'"

When Jesus asked this same question of His disciples many years ago, it was Simon Peter who gave the God-inspired answer: "You are the Christ, the Son of the living God" (Matthew 16:16).

By partaking of this memorial meal, we reaffirm that same, simple, age-old confession of faith: Jesus is the Christ, the Son of the living God. It is He who died on the cross for our sins, who arose from the dead, and who is coming again! He is our Lord and our Savior.

Date Used: _____

Covenant

Jesus used an important word when He first instituted the Lord's Supper, one that we frequently overlook. It is the word *covenant*. "And he said to them, 'This is my blood of the covenant, which is poured out for many'" (Mark 14:24).

Paul wrote, "In the same way also [Jesus took] the cup, after supper, saying, 'This cup is the new covenant in my blood. Do this, as often as you drink it, in remembrance of me'" (1 Corinthians 11:25).

A covenant is an agreement between two parties.

God has agreed to give us forgiveness and eternal life. He has sealed this agreement or covenant with the blood of His Son.

"Therefore he is the mediator of a new covenant, so that those who are called may receive the promised eternal inheritance, since a death has occurred which redeems them from the transgressions under the first covenant. For where a will is involved, the death of the one who made it must be established" (Hebrews 9:15, 16).

Jesus' death has been established and the new covenant is now in effect. What is your part of the agreement? To give Him your life and to live by faith in the Son of God.

This Communion is our reminder that we have made an agreement with God and are living in a covenant relationship with Him.

Date Used: _____

Cross

If you were asked to name or describe something that you felt was truly glorious, what would be it? A sunrise over the Grand Canyon? The surge of the ocean against a palm-lined beach on a clear summer's day? The majestic peaks of snow-capped mountains? One perfect rose? Love?

Who would think of mentioning anything so horrible and replusive as an object of terror, torture and death? Yet Paul wrote, "But far be it from me to glory except in the cross of our Lord Jesus Christ, by which the world has been crucified to me, and I to the world" (Galatians 6:14).

13

When you think of the experience of crucifixion, you can hardly describe it as being glorious. The cross was a horrible means of torturing a man to death. The pain was intense, the suffering constant, the thirst unbearable, and the humiliation unspeakable. It was an agonizing way to die. Yet Paul called it glorious.

But it was not the appearance of the cross or the event of the crucifixion to which he was referring. Rather it was what Jesus' death on the cross accomplished—our redemption. What a truly glorious thing God has done for us through the cross of Christ!

> "In the cross of Christ I glory,
> Towering o'er the wrecks of time;
> All the light of sacred story
> Gathers round its head sublime."

Date Used: _____

Death

In *Parallel Lives* by Plutarch, better known as *Plutarch's Lives*, the stories and military accomplishments of many of the ancient Greek and Roman heroes are recounted, men like Pompey, Caesar, Brutus, and Marc Antony.

It is interesting to note their response during times of war to the messengers who brought them news of the battle. If the news was good, they would often lavishly reward the messenger with houses, lands and money. If the news was bad, they might have the messenger executed.

Isn't it strange that Jesus came bearing good news and yet we still had Him executed? Perhaps even stranger still is the fact that His execution has become central to the good news itself!

"For we know that Christ being raised from the dead will never die again; death no longer has dominion over him. The death he died he died to sin, once for all, but the life he lives he lives to God. So you also must consider yourselves dead to sin and alive to God in Christ Jesus" (Romans 6:9-11).

The good news about Jesus' death is this: now we can die to sin and rise to walk in the newness of life. That is one of the meanings of baptism.

"We were buried therefore with him by baptism into death, so that as Christ was raised from the dead by the glory of the Father, we too might walk in newness of life" (Romans 6:4).

In this memorial meal we not only celebrate the death and resurrection of Jesus Christ, but our own death and resurrection as well!

Date Used: _____

Discipleship

"And he called to him the multitude with his disciples, and said to them, 'If any man would come after me, let him deny himself and take up his cross and follow me" (Mark 8:34).

Being a disciple of Jesus means being a cross-bearer. But that is no easy matter.

Before the performance of the Oberammergau Passion Play, a tourist was curiously looking around at the various props. Knowing something about how fake props are made, he smiled when he saw the cross lying on the pavement. But when he leaned over to pick it up, its weight surprised him.

"I thought it was surely hollow," he said to the actor standing nearby. But the Christ-actor replied, "You cannot play the part of Jesus and carry a light cross. You have to feel the full weight of it if you would feel the presence of the Master."

For Jesus the cross meant fulfilling His mission on earth even though it would mean suffering and death. To be His disciple means to bear your cross and to fulfill the mission to which God has called you, no matter what the cost.

Date Used: _____

Doubt

Jesus said, "Have faith in God. Truly, I say to you, whoever says to this mountain, 'Be taken up and cast into the sea, and does not doubt in his heart, but believes that what he says will come to pass, it will be done for him" (Mark 11:22, 23).

Wouldn't it be great to have that kind of faith? Yet it seems that to doubt is human. Even Thomas, one of the twelve who was right there on the scene, had his doubts.

"Unless I see in his hands the print of the nails," Thomas said, "and place my finger in the mark of the nails, and place my hand in his side, I will not believe" (John 20:25b). He sincerely doubted. But after he had seen the risen Lord he declared, "My Lord and my God!"

"Jesus said to him, 'Have you believed because you

have seen me? Blessed are those who have not seen and yet believe'" (John 20:28b, 29).

Let us lay aside our doubts and come to this table with the faith of a little child, simply believing that Jesus is the Son of God and that He died on the cross for our sins. We come without demanding special proof, signs, or miracles, but only with the prayer, "I believe; help my unbelief!" (Mark 9:24b)

Date Used: _____

Faith

Do you ever have the feeling that the weight of the world is on your shoulders and you just can't take it much longer? That burdens are too heavy, decisions too difficult, temptations too great, disappointments too frequent, or hurts too many?

The good news is that on the cross Jesus overcame the world, and now, you can too! "In the world you have tribulation," said Jesus, "but be of good cheer, I have overcome the world" (John 16:33b).

This is one of the reasons we talk about "celebrating" the Lord's Supper. This is a time to celebrate and to "be of good cheer," for by faith in Jesus we have a Savior who gives us victory over sin and death and the world and all of the hurt and futility that goes with it.

"For whatever is born of God overcomes the world; and this is the victory that overcomes the world, our faith. Who is it that overcomes the world but he who believes that Jesus is the Son of God?" (1 John 5:4, 5)

Date Used: _____

Forgiveness

To receive forgiveness, you must first give forgiveness.

From the cross, Jesus said to His enemies, "Father, forgive them; for they know not what they do" (Luke 23:34a). He offered forgiveness, but I wonder if they accepted it? Their response was, "They cast lots to divide his garments" (Luke 23:34b), as if they were totally unaware of what He had said.

Forgiveness is not automatic; you must be receptive to it. An unforgiving spirit will prevent God's forgiveness from taking place in your life.

Jesus taught us to pray, "Forgive us our debts, as we also have forgiven our debtors" (Matthew 6:12). Then he added this commentary: "For if you forgive men their trespasses, your heavenly Father also will forgive you; but if you do not forgive men their trespasses, neither will your Father forgive your trespasses" (Matthew 6:14, 15).

Perhaps we are more aware of how much we need God's forgiveness than we are of how much we need to be in the business of forgiving others.

First let us forgive any and all who have offended us or sinned against us in any way. Then let us seek and enjoy the forgiveness that Christ offers us from the cross.

Date Used: _____

Free From Sin

The prisoner's face was only partially visible through the small, thick pane of wire-reinforced glass. The speaker system was faulty and communication was difficult.

He was a believer and a member of the church who had gotten into drugs, or rather they had gotten into him. Now he was a prisoner of a habit as well as of the county.

There was essentially one question on his mind—what was being done to get him out of jail and into a drug rehabilitation program? He wanted to be free on both accounts and he was willing to do whatever was necessary. Over and over again he stressed that anything would be better than imprisonment. He wanted to be free!

Real and lasting freedom comes through obedience to Jesus. "The Lord sets the prisoners free" (Psalms 146:7b). Absolute freedom is a myth; there is no such thing. True freedom is found in obeying laws and accepting limitations and honoring boundaries. To be free from sin means to become a bond-servant of Jesus Christ.

"Do you not know that if you yield yourselves to any one as obedient slaves, you are slaves of the one whom you obey, either of sin, which leads to death, or of obedience, which leads to righteousness? But thanks be to God, that you who were once slaves of sin have become obedient from the heart to the standard of teaching to which you were committed, and, having been set free from sin, have becomes slaves of righteousness" (Romans 6:16-18).

Christ's death on the cross frees us *from* sin and death, and it frees us *to* worship and service.

Date Used: _____

Grace

Grace Is Not a Blue-Eyed Blond is the clever title of one book about the grace of God.

But what is grace? Here are a few revealing definitions selected from a "collegiate" dictionary:

1. elegance or beauty of form, manner, motion, or action;
2. favor or good will;
3. a manifestation of favor, especially by a superior;
4. mercy, clemency, pardon; and,
5. the freely given, unmerited favor and love of God.

The apostle Paul has given us this beautiful and elegant explanation of God's grace: "He destined us in love to be his sons through Jesus Christ, according to the purpose of his will, to the praise of his glorious grace which he freely bestowed on us in the Beloved. In him we have redemption through his blood, the forgiveness of our trespasses, according to the riches of his grace which he lavished upon us" (Ephesians 1:5-8).

At this table we remember and give thanks to God for this great and wonderful grace.

Date Used: _____

Guilt

"Every one who commits sin is guilty of lawlessness; sin is lawlessness" (1 John 3:4). Guilty! All of us have experienced guilt because all of us have committed sin. Guilt is that negative feeling that results not only from breaking laws but also from violating relationships.

We must deal with the problem of guilt. Unattended it produces feelings of inadequacy, low self-esteem, separation from others, fear, depression, and even suicide.

Guilt is God's gift to us. It warns us when we get off track, do wrong, hurt someone, or disobey. It causes our soul to cry out for forgiveness and reconciliation, as David did in Psalm 51.

"Create in me a clean heart, O God,
   and put a new and right spirit within me.
Cast me not away from thy presence,
   and take not thy holy Spirit from me.
Deliver me from bloodguiltiness, O God,
   thou God of my salvation,
   and my tongue will sing aloud of thy deliverance.
The sacrifice acceptable to God is a broken spirit;
   a broken and contrite heart, O God, thou wilt not
   despise,"   (Psalms 51:10, 11, 14, 17).

Jesus' death on the cross is God's answer to the problem of guilt and to the prayers of the penitent. Through Christ He delivers us, cleanses us, and restores us to fellowship with himself.

It is Jesus "who will sustain you to the end, guiltless in the day of our Lord Jesus Christ" (1 Corinthians 1:8).

Date Used: _____

Humility

"God opposes the proud, but gives grace to the humble." Therefore, "Humble yourselves before the Lord and he will exalt you" (James 4:6b, 10).

Following his coronation, king George III was to receive the Lord's Supper after the usual tradition.

When it was offered to him he said he would not accept it wearing the crown. So he removed his crown and asked the queen to do the same.

With some embarrassment she explained that this would be difficult to do, since hers was pinned on. So the king announced, "Then let it be understood that her Majesty received the Lord's Supper not as a queen, but as a Christian."

Our greatest example, however, is that of the King of kings.

"Have this mind among yourselves, which is yours in Christ Jesus, who, though he was in the form of God, did not count equality with God a thing to be grasped, but emptied himself, taking the form of a servant, being born in the likeness of men. And being found in human form he humbled himself and became obedient unto death, even death on a cross" (Philippians 2:5-8).

The humility and death of Christ is the example that God wants us to follow in our relationship with one another.

Date Used: _____

Joy

There is joy in obedience. Hebrews 12:2 refers to Jesus as "the pioneer and perfecter of our faith, who for the joy that was set before him endured the cross, despising the shame, and is seated at the right hand of the throne of God."

The cross was both painful and shameful. But the joy came in Christ's knowing that He was doing God's will by dying for our sins.

Games are more fun when played by the rules.

When rules are ignored, broken, or changed there are more arguments and fights (as I recall from my experience playing Monopoly). The result is chaos, and that is no fun at all. Some games, such as sports, would become dangerous if not deadly.

The game of life is like that. God has given us rules and commandments for the sake of our own joy. Jesus said, "If you keep my commandments, you will abide in my love, just as I have kept my Father's commandments and abide in his love. These things I have spoken to you, that my joy may be in you, and that your joy may be full" (John 15:10, 11).

Jesus played by the rules, even though it meant death on the cross, but had the joy of winning our salvation. Now He calls us to joyful obedience.

Date Used: _____

Judgment

"Whoever, therefore, eats the bread or drinks the cup of the Lord in an unworthy manner will be guilty of profaning the body and blood of the Lord. Let a man examine himself, and so eat of the bread and drink of the cup. For any one who eats and drinks without discerning the body eats and drinks judgment upon himself. That is why many of you are weak and ill, and some have died" (1 Corinthians 11:27-30).

How seriously do you take this time in our worship service? Is your participation mechanical and routine, or do you deliberately and consciously meditate on the significance of what we are doing here?

Abuse of this meal brings judgment. The Lord's Supper is abused when it is taken "in an unworthy manner," lightly or casually or irreverently. It is abused when one fails to "examine himself," with introspection and confession and repentance. It is abused if one partakes "without discerning the body," thoughtlessly, carelessly, neglecting the fact that this represents the broken body and the shed blood of our Lord.

The Lord's Supper deserves thoughtful, concentrated meditation. God's judgment is a fearful thing!

"How much worse punishment do you think will be deserved by the man who has spurned the Son of God, and profaned the blood of the covenant by which he was sanctified, and outraged the Spirit of grace? For we know him who said, 'Vengeance is mine, I will repay.' And again, 'The Lord will judge his people.' It is a fearful thing to fall into the hands of the living God" (Hebrews 10:29-31).

Date Used: _____

Love

The Lord's Supper is like a work of art. Here in the bread and the cup we see a portrait of the body and the blood of Jesus. Our mind's eye pictures Him hanging on the cross, dying for our sins.

Like any good art, however, there is more in these emblems than mere form and color. There is also a message. The famous German poet and dramatist, Goethe (go-tuh), once observed that "the highest cannot be spoken."

The Lord's Supper says something about the love of God for sinful man that cannot be put into words. But it was put into action, in Christ's death upon the cross.

And now that message has been put into this memorial meal so that we will never forget.

"Greater love has no man than this, that a man lay down his life for his friends" (John 15:13).

Date Used: _____

Love One Another

"Beloved, let us love one another; for love is of God, and he who loves is born of God and knows God. He who does not love does not know God; for God is love" (1 John 4:7, 8).

In his play, *The Amen Corner*, James Baldwin tells about Sister Margaret, a black woman who literally takes over as the pastor of a storefront church in a Harlem ghetto in New York City. She seems intent on power and control and doesn't mind manipulating people in order to get her way.

But then things begin to go wrong. Her son, who plays the piano for the little congregation, can't "feel the spirit" anymore and deserts her. Her alcoholic and unfaithful husband returns to her ill and dies. Through all of this the congregation loses faith in her and decides to vote her out.

On her last Sunday, Sister Margaret plans to tell them off good. But as she steps to the pulpit she has a change of heart and realizes how wrong she has been. In an unusually quiet voice she speaks to her people.

"Children, I'm just now finding out what it means to love the Lord. It ain't all in the singing and the shouting. It ain't all in the reading of the Bible. It ain't even . . . it ain't even . . . in running all over everybody trying to get to heaven. To love the Lord is to love all his children, all of them, every one, and to suffer with them and never count the cost!" Then silently she turns and leaves.

"In this is love, not that we loved God but that he loved us and sent his Son to be the expiation for our sins. Beloved, if God so loved us, we also ought to love one another" (1 John 4:10, 11).

Date Used: _____

Purpose

She was five years old and watched intently as her father took Communion. After eating the little piece of bread and drinking the small cup of grape juice, he immediately lowered his head in meditation, aware that she was staring at him.

She nudged him but he ignored her. Then she nudged him again, a little harder this time. As quietly as possible he whispered, "What is it?"

"Daddy," she asked softly, "what did that do to you?"

How would you have answered?

A better, and perhaps easier, question would be, "What does that mean to you?" We can find several important meanings in 1 Corinthians 11:23-29.

The Lord's Supper means:

1. Thanksgiving: "when he had given thanks" (v. 24)
2. Christ's presence: "This is my body" (v. 24)
3. Obedience: "Do this" (v. 24)
4. Remembering: "in remembrance of me" (v. 24)
5. Covenant: "This cup is the new covenant in my blood" (v. 25)
6. Proclamation: "you proclaim the Lord's death until he comes" (v. 26)

7. Self-examination: "Let a man examine himself" (v. 28)

8. Discernment: "discerning the body" (v. 29)

Through this Scripture God is gently nudging us and asking, "What does it mean to you?"

Date Used: _____

Remembrance

"For I received from the Lord what I also delivered to you, that the Lord Jesus on the night when he was betrayed took bread, and when he had given thanks, he broke it, and said, 'This is my body which is for you. Do this in remembrance of me'" (1 Corinthians 11:23, 24).

The last meal that Jesus had with His apostles was the Passover meal (Matthew 26:17f). During this meal they would eat unleavened bread, drink unfermented wine and eat specially prepared lamb. They would remember the slavery in Egypt, the blood of the lamb on the doorposts, and the passing over of the death angel. It was a memorial meal designed by God to help them remember their deliverance out of bondage and into the promised land.

It was this bread and this "fruit of the vine" that Jesus used to institute a new memorial meal that we now call the Lord's Supper. It is to remind God's people today of deliverance from slavery to sin, of the blood of the Lamb of God upon the cross, and of our redemption from Hell—the second death.

The bread reminds us of His broken body. The cup reminds us of His shed blood. The meal reminds us our sins have been forgiven and that one day we shall enter that new, promised land called Heaven. Let us remember, and give thanks.

Date Used: _____

Repentance

God abhors sin, but He delights in repentance. King David understood this. "The sacrifice acceptable to God is a broken spirit; a broken and contrite heart, O God, thou wilt not despise" (Psalms 51:17).

Jesus taught this. "Just so, I tell you, there will be more joy in heaven over one sinner who repents than over ninety-nine righteous persons who need no repentance" (Luke 15:7). He also clearly taught the necessity of repentance. "Unless you repent you will all likewise perish" (Luke 13:3).

To repent means to change. It means to have a change of heart, mind, direction, and behavior. Repentance is a decision one makes regarding sin. It is saying, "I am sorry I have sinned. I do not want to continue in sin. Now I want to obey God and live for Him."

The Lord's Supper is a time for us to look carefully into our own lives and behavior. Any sin that we discover there must be confessed to God in humble repentance. His promise is to cleanse and to forgive.

"If we confess our sins, he is faithful and just, and will forgive our sins and cleanse us from all unrighteousness" (1 John 1:9).

Date Used: _____

Sacrifice

Henry Van Dyke tells about a political prisoner during the French Revolution who was very much loved by the people, but especially by his father. The two men bore a resemblance and had exactly the same name.

When the son's name was called for him to step forward to be executed, the father went up instead. He willingly placed his head on the block and the great blade of the guillotine was dropped. Through his sacrifice his son was free to live and carry on his work.

This is like Christ's love for you. You are the one who is guilty of sin. Your name has been called in judgment. But Christ has stepped forward to take your punishment and to die in your place. Now you are free to live!

"Surely he has borne our griefs
    and carried our sorrows;
yet we esteemed him stricken,
    smitten by God, and afflicted.
But he was wounded for our transgressions,
    he was bruised for our iniquities;
upon him was the chastisement that made us whole,
    and with his stripes we are healed.
All we like sheep have gone astray;
    we have turned every one to his own way;
and the Lord has laid on him
the iniquity of us all."

(Isaiah 53:4-6)

Date Used: _____

Salvation

"Blessed be the Lord,
    who daily bears us up;
    God is our salvation.
Our God is a God of salvation;
    and to God, the Lord, belongs
    escape from death."
              (Psalms 68:19, 20)

From what does God save us? From sin, with all of its treachery and its power to enslave us. From guilt, with its heavy burden of fear, despondency, and defeatism. From death and Hell, the second death that separates one from God for all eternity.

God's salvation enables us to enjoy life. We can live life with confidence and hope and with the assurance that in Christ, life is everlasting. His salvation frees us for love, worship, and service.

Our God is a great God. Prophecy has been fulfilled and our prayers have been answered. "She will bear a son, and you shall call his name Jesus, for he will save his people from their sins" (Matthew 1:21).

Date Used: _____

Self-Examination

"When it was evening, he sat at table with the twelve disciples; and as they were eating, he said, 'Truly, I say to you, one of you will betray me.' And they were very sorrowful, and began to say to him one after another, 'Is it I, Lord?'" (Matthew 26:20-22).

The Lord's Supper is no quick road to spiritual

ecstacy, no easy way out of your personal hang-ups. Rather, it is a moment of truth, a time for confrontation. Here is where you must search deeply for your innermost self, asking God that often self-condemning question, "Lord, is it I?"

Will you, like Judas, eat this meal under false pretenses? Will you declare at this table that you are a friend of God and a blood brother of Jesus Christ, only to leave this place and later deny that you even know Him, perhaps betray Him for the sake of getting along with the crowd?

This meal cannot casually be eaten. Either you make a commitment to the Host of this table and pledge Him your love and loyalty, or else you perform a lie and eat and drink judgment against yourself.

The latter is what Judas did. When he realized it he could no longer live with himself, so he committed suicide.

"Let a man examine himself, and so eat of the bread and drink of the cup. For any one who eats and drinks without discerning the body eats and drinks judgment upon himself" (1 Corinthians 11:28, 29).

Date Used: _____

Sin

Sin means "missing the mark." The "mark" or target that we are aiming for is the glory of God, His perfect will, which we all have missed. "All have sinned and fall short of the glory of God" (Romans 3:23).

Sin is disobedience. It is doing things God has told us not to do and not doing things that He has told us to do.

Disbelief is also sin, perhaps the greatest sin, and ignorance is no excuse.

Sin is deceptive. It offers beauty, pleasure, and fulfillment, but produces ugliness, disappointment, and emptiness. Sin is guilty of false advertising; it thrives on lies. Yet there are many who think that temptation to sin is irresistible.

Sin is destructive. It is a cancer on society and on the human soul. It destroys individuals, marriages, friendships, and families. One day it will reap the destruction of the world. It is habit-forming and has the power to enslave, so that those who think they are in control of sinful habits are soon controlled by them.

Worst of all, sin separates man from God. To sin is to side with the enemy whose ultimate destruction is certain. Sin represents all that man hates and wants to avoid. It keeps him from being what he wants to be and what God has created him to be.

The good news is that this terrible enemy has been defeated. By God's grace, through Christ's death on the cross, we are set free from sin and its hold over us. It is that forgiveness and that freedom that we celebrate here at the Lord's table.

"Let not sin therefore reign in your mortal bodies, to make you obey their passions. Do not yield your members to sin as instruments of wickedness, but yield yourselves to God as men who have been brought from death to life, and your members to God as instruments of righteousness. For sin will have no dominion over you, since you are not under law but under grace" (Romans 6:12-14).

Date Used: _____

Suffering

"Then the soldiers of the governor took Jesus into the praetorium, and they gathered the whole battalion before him. And they stripped him and put a scarlet robe upon him, and plaiting a crown of thorns they put it on his head, and put a reed in his right hand. And kneeling before him they mocked him, saying, 'Hail, King of the Jews!' And they spat upon him, and took the reed and struck him on the head. And when they had mocked him, they stripped him of the robe, and put his own clothes on him, and led him away to crucify him" (Matthew 27:27-31).

The story of the crucifixion of Jesus is a story of suffering. At the cross, Jesus suffered and died for us. His suffering was very real and very great. It is not easy to watch someone suffer, especially someone that you love. But look at Jesus and see how He suffered.

He suffered the physical pain and hurt of the scourging, of the thorns being pressed into the tender flesh of His scalp, of being slapped and struck with the reed, of the nails being driven through the flesh of His hands and feet, of the tearing of His flesh as the cross was jolted into its place.

He suffered the ordeal of injustice at an illegal trial, the betrayal and denial and silence of His own followers, the spittle and mockery of the soldiers, the constant pain of hanging on the cross, the terrible moment He was forsaken by His Father.

Why did He do it? The only answer is love. The suffering of Jesus convinces us of His love for us. There is no extreme to which He would not go, in order to love us and save us and draw us to himself.

Date Used: _____

Unity

In John 17 Jesus prays for the unity of all believers, "that they may all be one; even as thou, Father, art in me, and I in thee, that they also may be in us, so that the world may believe that thou hast sent me" (John 17:21).

At this table we celebrate the unity we have with God, with one another, and even within ourselves.

Sin has separated us from God, but Jesus' death on the cross has cleansed us of sin and reunited us with Him.

Sin has alienated us from one another, but Jesus' death on the cross has reconciled us and restored us to unity and brotherhood.

Sin has even destroyed the integrity within ourselves, but Jesus' death on the cross has brought us spiritual healing and renewed wholeness. In Him we have integrity.

We thank God for this unity, for it enables us to enjoy fellowship with Him and with one another, to experience peace within our own lives, and to present a unified and effective witness to others.

"But now in Christ Jesus you who were far off have been brought near in the blood of Christ. For he is our peace, who has made us both one, and has broken down the dividing wall of hostility, by abolishing in his flesh the law of commandments and ordinances, that he might create in himself one new man in place of the two, so making peace, and might reconcile us both to God in one body through the cross, thereby bringing the hostility to an end" (Ephesians 2:13-16).

Date Used: _____

Worship

Communion is central to the life and worship of the church. The Lord's Supper is an important and integral part of the worship service. That is because Jesus' death on the cross is at the heart of what it means to be a Christian.

Like worship, however, Communion with Christ is not limited to a Sunday morning worship service. Worship is something we do every day as we honor God with our work, our morals, our language, etc. Communion with Christ must also be a daily experience.

James D. Smart (in his book, *The Teaching Ministry of the Church*) explained it this way. "The bread of life that is offered in Word and sacrament in formal worship is bread for every day and every moment. The members of the Church do not cease to be the Church when they are scattered to their several occupations, and, whenever they are, they must feed continually upon the bread of life or they die.

"Our daily life is not life but rather death unless, in every hour of every day, we are the Church that abides in God and has God's Word abiding in it. Worship is the Church's vital breath."

The emblems we receive at this table are reminders of Christ's constant presence in our lives and of our constant need to abide in Him.

Jesus said, "Abide in me, and I in you. As the branch cannot bear fruit by itself, unless it abides in the vine, neither can you, unless you abide in me. I am the vine, you are the branches. He who abides in me, and I in him, he it is that bears much fruit, for apart from me you can do nothing" (John 15:4, 5).

Date Used: _____

Communion Meditations for Special Days

New Year's Day

Have you made your New Year's resolutions? Or have you given up on making them? Each year it seems to take us less time to come to the realization that our resolutions don't last long. It takes more than resolve to make a new start in life.

After a few years of broken resolutions we may begin to feel like the "preacher" of Ecclesiastes, who wrote: "What has been is what will be, and what has been done is what will be done; and there is nothing new under the sun" (Ecclesiastes 1:9).

Resolve is a good and necessary thing if only we can follow through on it. What is the solution to broken resolutions? Having the right resource that will enable you to succeed, where before you failed.

At this table we remember that it is Christ, not the turning of the page of a calendar, that makes a new beginning possible. It is not being in a new year, but being in Christ, that makes the difference.

As Paul put it, "Therefore, if any one is in Christ, he is a new creation; the old has passed away, behold, the new has come" (2 Corinthians 5:17).

Date Used: _____

Palm Sunday

Less than one week before His crucifixion, Jesus rode into Jerusalem on a colt with all the praise and pageantry accorded to a conquering hero or a king. It was a magnificent and spectacular occasion.

"Most of the crowd spread their garments on the road, and others cut branches from the trees and spread them on the road. And the crowds that went before him and that followed him shouted, 'Hosanna to the Son of David! Blessed is he who comes in the name of the Lord! Hosanna in the highest!' And when he entered Jerusalem, all the city was stirred, saying, 'Who is this?' And the crowds said, 'This is the prophet Jesus from Nazareth of Galilee'" (Matthew 21:8-11).

Evidently they did not yet have a clear understanding of His identity. They knew Him only as a prophet, rabbi, healer or miracle worker, but not as Messiah. Perhaps that is why they were so readily swayed a few days later and joined the crowds in demanding His execution.

Who is Jesus? Are you confused or doubtful concerning His true identity? Our praise is shallow and empty unless we understand, and are fully committed to the revelation, that He is the divine Son of God.

Date Used: _____

Easter

That Jesus of Nazareth once lived on earth and died upon a cross is documented as historical fact. So also is His resurrection from the dead. There were numerous and consistent eyewitness accounts that verify this fact.

Consider Paul's record, for example. "For I delivered to you as of first importance what I also received, that Christ died for our sins in accordance with the scriptures, that he was buried, that he was raised on the third day in accordance with the scriptures, and that he appeared to Cephas, then to the twelve. Then he appeared to more than five hundred brethren at one time, most of whom are still alive, though some have fallen asleep. Then he appeared to James, then to all the apostles. Last of all, as to one untimely born, he appeared also to me" (1 Corinthians 15:3-8).

Now compare this with what the Jewish historian, Josephus (c. 37-100 A.D.), wrote about Jesus in *Antiquities of the Jews.*

"Now, there was about this time, Jesus, a wise man, if it be lawful to call him a man, for he was a doer of wonderful works,—a teacher of such men as receive the truth with pleasure. He drew over to him both many of the Jews, and many of the Gentiles.

"He was [the] Christ; and when Pilate, at the suggestion of the principal men amongst us, had condemned him to the cross, those that loved him at the first did not forsake him, for he appeared to them alive again the third day, as the divine prophets had foretold these and ten thousand other wonderful things concerning him; and the tribe of Christians, so named from him, are not extinct at this day" (*Antiquities* III.3).

Josephus was a Jew and a Pharisee, and evidently remained so throughout his life, although he was fully aware of, and recorded as historical fact, the resurrection of Jesus from the dead. Why was he unaffected by this great truth?

Fact, without faith, is futile. You can know and believe the facts regarding Jesus' life, death, *and* resurrection and still not trust in Him as your personal Lord and Savior.

It is not just the fact of Easter that we celebrate this morning. Rather, it is our personal relationship with our risen and living Lord that brings us to this table.

Date Used: _____

Mother's Day

One of Jesus' seven last sayings from the cross had to do with His mother, Mary. While He was hanging on the cross, suffering, bleeding, agonizing over the sins of the world, He remembered His mother.

"Standing by the cross of Jesus were his mother, and his mother's sister, Mary the wife of Clopas, and Mary Magdalene. When Jesus saw his mother, and the disciple whom he loved standing near, he said to his mother, "Woman, behold, your son!" Then he said to the disciple, "Behold, your mother!" And from that hour the disciple took her to his own home" (John 19:25-27).

We assume that Joseph was no longer living and that Mary, therefore, had no place to go, or at least no plans. What a terrible ordeal for her! Watching the son to whom she had given birth being brutally tortured to death, writhing in agony on a cruel Roman cross.

But in the midst of His pain and suffering, Jesus remembered his mother. His words thoughtfully commended her to John's care. John understood this, and accepted the responsibility of caring for Mary the rest of her life.

Today we remember Christ on the cross. We remember that His body was broken and His blood was shed so that we might have forgiveness of sins and life everlasting. But we also remember that He remembered His mother.

Date Used: _____

Children's Day/Youth Sunday

We take pride in our children, although there are times when we may be embarrassed by their behavior.

We are for our children, although there are times when we may become impatient with them and perhaps do not care for them as we should.

We love our children, although there are times when we may barely be able to tolerate them.

Jesus wants us to see more in our relationship with our children than how we may feel about them or our responsibility to them. He wants us to see that their lives provide an important example for us.

"At that time the disciples came to Jesus, saying, 'Who is the greatest in the kingdom of heaven?' And calling to him a child, he put him in the midst of them, and said, 'Truly, I say to you, unless you turn and become like children, you will never enter the kingdom of heaven. Whoever humbles himself like this child, he is the greatest in the kingdom of heaven'" (Matthew 18:1-4).

Greatness, according to God, is not material success or personal achievement or having power over others.

It is childlikeness. It is learning and exemplifying in our lives those childlike qualities of faith, trust and humility.

Christ on the cross gave us the perfect example of what He was talking about. "Who, though he was in the form of God, did not count equality with God a thing to be grasped, but emptied himself, taking the form of a servant, being born in the likeness of men. And being found in human form he humbled himself and became obedient unto death, even death on a cross" (Philippians 2:6-8).

Date Used: ___ _____

Memorial Day

Have you ever been forgotten? That it was your birthday or anniversary? Or that you were to be picked up at a certain time or met at a certain place? And somebody that you were counting on simply forgot! You were probably disappointed, hurt, and perhaps even angry.

It is important to remember. That is why we have so many reminders—a birthday card, an anniversary present, a calendar book, a ring on the finger. These things remind us of important events. But even more important is that they remind us of people and relationships.

The wedding ring is a reminder of the day when we first put it on with the solemn promise, "till death do us part." It is not only a reminder of yesterday, but also a reminder for today and tomorrow and until death. It reminds us of the event of our wedding, but also of the ongoing relationship of our marriage.

41

This memorial meal is also a reminder of a past event and of a present relationship. The event is Jesus' death on the cross almost two thousand years ago. The relationship is Christ in you and you in Him, both now and forever. It is important that we partake of these emblems and remember.

Date Used: _____

Father's Day

"Honor your father. . . ." That is God's will for your life. It is recorded in both the Old and New Testaments.

The best way to honor your father is to do those things that will please him: take him the newspaper, fix him a special meal, compliment him on his work, introduce him to your friends, write him a letter of appreciation, give him a gift, tell him, "I love you, Dad."

What pleases a father most of all, however, is for his son or his daughter to grow up to be the kind of person he has hoped and prayed and worked for them to be.

Jesus was that kind of Son to His Father, God. He honored His Father by living His life pleasing to God, by doing His Father's will. God's will and purpose for Jesus was to reconcile all men to himself by His sacrifice upon the cross. Jesus wrestled with that decision, but He submitted.

"My Father," Jesus prayed in the garden of Gethsemane, "if it be possible, let this cup pass from me; nevertheless, not as I will, but as thou wilt" (Matthew 26:39).

We thank Jesus at this table for His humble obedience to His Father's will and for dying on the cross for our sins. Here let us also renew our commitments to live our lives pleasing unto God, our heavenly Father.

Date Used: _____

Pentecost

Today is the birthday of the church. It was on the Jewish feast day of Pentecost, just fifty days following Christ's resurrection, that the church was born. The record of its beginning is in Acts, chapter two.

On this day the Holy Spirit was poured out upon the apostles and they began to speak in other tongues (v. 4). Men from many different countries heard them speaking, each in his own language (v. 6).

On this day Peter explained to the masses in Jerusalem that what they were witnessing was a fulfillment of the prophet Joel, who said: "And in the last days it shall be, God declares, that I will pour out my Spirit upon all flesh . . ." (v. 17a).

On this day the first recorded gospel sermon was preached, and it included these simple, timeless truths: "This Jesus, delivered up according to the definite plan and foreknowledge of God, you crucified and killed by the hands of lawless men. But God raised him up, having loosed the pangs of death, because it was not possible for him to be held by it" (vv. 23, 24).

On this day those who were cut to the heart by this message wanted to know what to do; "And Peter said to them, 'Repent, and be baptized every one of you in the name of Jesus Christ for the forgiveness of your sins; and you shall receive the gift of the Holy Spirit" (v. 38).

And it was on this day that "those who received his word were baptized, and there were added that day about three thousand souls. And they devoted themselves to the apostles' teaching and fellowship, to the breaking of bread and the prayers" (vv. 41, 42).

Today as a Christian church we celebrate our birthday by meeting together on the first day of the week for the same purposes that were there when the church first began. Let us give God thanks for the church, and for the head of the church, Jesus Christ.

Date Used: _____

Independence Day

"The Lord sets the prisoners free" (Psalms 146:7b). People from many lands have found political freedom here in America to worship as they choose. That freedom has often been abused, yet it is one we greatly cherish, because it means we can assemble for worship and give open expression to our faith in God.

Even more important is the spiritual freedom we have in Christ, a freedom that people everywhere can know and enjoy whatever the political climate may be. "For freedom Christ has set us free; stand fast therefore, and do not submit again to a yoke of slavery" (Galatians 5:1).

This freedom was made possible by Christ's death on the cross. He has set us free from bondage to the law and its power, which is sin and death. This freedom becomes ours personally when we put our faith in Jesus and are obedient to Him.

We maintain this freedom through proper use of it. "For you were called to freedom, brethren; only do not use your freedom as an opportunity for the flesh, but through love be servants of one another" (Galatians

5:13). We are not free to sin; we are free to love and to serve one another!

We come to this table to remember the price that was paid for our freedom—Jesus' death upon the cross— and to give thanks.

Date Used: _____

Labor Day

Labor Day is a popular holiday if for no other reason than getting a day off from work. We usually enjoy not working. We like to take vacation from work. We are even tempted sometimes to call in sick when we don't really feel bad just so we don't have to go in to work.

The truth is that we need to work and would be quite empty without it—at least until retirement! Work enables us to be productive, serve others, and provide for our families. It is also part of our obedience to God: "If any one will not work, let him not eat" (2 Thessalonians 3:10b).

However, earning a living is not to be the focal point of all our labors. Jesus said, 'Do not labor for the food which perishes, but for the food which endures to eternal life, which the Son of man will give to you; for on him has God the Father set his seal.' Then they said to him, 'What must we do, to be doing the works of God?' Jesus answered them, 'This is the work of God, that you believe in him whom he has sent'" (John 6:27-29).

Our primary work on earth is faith in God, with all that faith implies: worshiping God, imitating Jesus, loving one another, preaching the gospel, helping those in need.

This time of Communion with Christ helps us to keep our primary purpose here on earth in perspective, and to remember that He is first in our lives and in our labors.

Date Used: _____

Thanksgiving

"Rejoice always, pray constantly, give thanks in all circumstances; for this is the will of God in Christ Jesus for you" (1 Thessalonians 5:16-18). God's will for you is to rejoice and pray and give thanks at all times and in all circumstances. Do you do that?

As unusual monument was constructed and placed on the courthouse square in Enterprise, Alabama. It was not to a founding father or a war hero, but to an insect, the Mexican boll weevil.

In 1895 this little town was nearly wiped off the map by the destructive force of the boll weevil. The cotton crop, on which the town thrived, was ruined.

Rather than give up and die, the farmers chose to diversify. They planted other crops, especially peanuts. Today Enterprise is a thriving little city known as "The Peanut Capital of the World." So they have honored and given thanks for the adversity brought to them by the boll weevil.

The prophet Habakkuk was of the same mind when he wrote:

> "Though the fig tree do not blossom,
> nor fruit be on the vines,
> the produce of the olive fail
> and the fields yield no food,

the flock be cut off from the fold
and there be no herd in the stalls,
yet I will rejoice in the Lord,
I will joy in the God of my salvation"
(Habakkuk 3:17, 18).

For the cross of Christ, for adverse circumstances in our own lives, for all things, let us give thanks.

Date Used: _____

Christmas

There are so many people today who celebrate Christmas yet who have a total disregard for its meaning and its message. But it has been that way from the beginning. "He came to his own home, and his own people received him not" (John 1:11).

Several years ago the Colorado Bureau of Investigation sent this directive to law enforcement agencies across the state: "Fortunately, the message we asked you to disregard was not sent. Thus, we ask that you disregard the message we sent asking you to disregard the last message."

If the world has tempted you to disregard the message of Christmas, then kindly disregard that message. What has God communicated to us through the coming of Christ into the world? John has stated the message of Christmas with beauty and inspiration. From John, chapter one:

"In the beginning was the Word, and the Word was with God, and the Word was God" (v. 1).

"And the Word became flesh and dwelt among us, full of grace and truth; we have beheld his glory, glory as of the only Son from the Father" (v. 14).

"No one has ever seen God; the only Son, who is in the bosom of the Father, he has made him known" (v. 18).

Do not disregard this message! Christmas means the birth of Christ, the coming of God, the gift of a Savior!

"But to all who received him, who believed in his name, he gave power to become children of God" (v. 12).

Date Used: _____

Communion Meditations for Special Occasions

Anniversary of the Congregation

How old is the church? It is as old as the day that Jesus told his disciples, ". . . and on this rock I will build my church, and the powers of death [or the gates of Hades] shall not prevail against it" (Matthew 16:18b).

Some time ago *Parade* magazine related a news item about a five-year-old boy whose goldfish died. He asked his friend, the lady next door, to help him prepare an epitaph for the grave marker. "What do you want me to write?" she asked.

"His name was Mobert," the youngster replied.

"Is there anything else?"

After thinking about it a moment he added, "Put, 'He was fun while he lasted.'"

We can and should enjoy the fellowship of the church. But our commitment to it is not based on "while the fun lasts." Rather, our church membership is based upon our commitment to the Lord of the church, Jesus Christ.

When we become Christians, we become members of Christ's body, the church. That is a relationship which God intends to be permanent and eternal—the very power of death and the gates of Hell cannot prevail against it.

At this table we remember that Christ is the head of the church, which He has bought with His own blood, and we are members of His body. Let us give thanks.

Date Used: _____

Baptismal Service

"Jesus answered, 'Truly, truly, I say to you, unless one is born of water and the Spirit, he cannot enter the kingdom of God'" (John 3:5). In baptism we are born of water and the Spirit and become members of Christ and His family, the church. That means we also belong to one another.

"For just as the body is one and has many members, and all the members of the body, though many, are one body, so it is with Christ. For by one Spirit we were all baptized into one body—Jews or Greeks, slaves or free—and all were made to drink of one Spirit" (1 Corinthians 12:12, 13).

This union that we enjoy with Christ, and therefore with one another, is seen and celebrated each time we partake of the Lord's Supper. It reminds us that we belong to each other because we belong to Him.

"The cup of blessing which we bless, is it not a participation in the blood of Christ? The bread which we break, is it not a participation in the body of Christ? Because there is one bread, we who are many are one body, for we all partake of the one bread" (1 Corinthians 10:16, 17).

Let us give thanks for this newly baptized member of our church family, for one another, and for Jesus Christ, who by His death upon the cross has made our salvation possible.

Date Used: _____

Camp Retreat

"You have been born anew, not of perishable seed but of imperishable, through the living and abiding word of God; for

'All flesh is like grass
    and all its glory like the flower of grass.
The grass withers, and the flower falls,
    but the word of the Lord abides for ever.'
That word is the good news which was
    preached to you" (1 Peter 1:23-25).

God's creation is beautiful and enjoyable. It is good to get out of doors where you can really see and appreciate nature. But it will all die and pass away, and that is sad. That is because it comes from perishable seed. The grass will wither and die, the flowers will wilt from the summer heat or freeze from the winter chill; the earth is being eroded and the air polluted; animals kill animals and man kills man. All creation will pass away.

Man is God's special creation, but God's Word reminds us that "all flesh is like grass." Its glory will fade and it, too, shall pass away. The mortician applies cosmetics to the cadaver but the beauty is no longer there;

the glory has already faded. And with death comes decay.

True beauty is to be found in the lives of those who have been born of the imperishable seed, God's new creation. There will someday be a new Heaven and a new earth and all God's people will enjoy it forever, and there will be no death there.

These emblems remind us of Jesus' sacrifice on the cross for our sins. This is our point of new beginning. "Therefore, if any one is in Christ, he is a new creation; the old has passed away, behold, the new has come" (2 Corinthians 5:17).

Date Used: _____

Dedication of a New Building

"So with yourselves; since you are eager for manifestations of the Spirit, strive to excel in building up the church" (1 Corinthians 14:12). God wants us to be excellent church builders.

We have attempted to do our best through the building of these facilities, and have dedicated them to the glory of God and for His purposes. But it is essential that we excel in building up the church that is His body—in other words, in building up each other.

One of the ways to do this is by coming together for fellowship, doctrine, the breaking of bread, and prayer. "Let us consider how to stir up one another to love and good works, not neglecting to meet together, as is the habit of some, but encouraging one another, and all the more as you see the Day drawing near" (Hebrews 10:24, 25).

An excellent way to build up the church is to meet

together in Christian fellowship, to pray for one another, and to break bread together as the family of God, as we do now at this table.

Date Used: _____

Musical Concert/Choir Cantata

God has given us the gift of music and is surely pleased when we use that gift for His glory and honor, as we have witnessed here today.

When we all get to Heaven, the old hymn says, we'll sing and shout the victory! Even those of us who don't sing so well will be included in that heavenly choir, and maybe even play on a harp! At least that is the preview we see through John's vision in the book of Revelation.

"And when he had taken the scroll, the four living creatures and the twenty-four elders fell down before the Lamb, each holding a harp, and with golden bowls full of incense, which are the prayers of the saints; and they sang a new song, saying,

> "Worthy art thou to take the scroll
>   and to open its seals,
> for thou wast slain and by the blood
>   didst ransom men for God
> from every tribe and tongue
>   and people and nation,
> and hast made them a kingdom
>   and priests to our God,
> and they shall reign on earth"
>   (Revelation 5:8-10)

The song to be sung (with harp accompaniment) is the old, old, story. By the blood of the Lamb we have been saved and by His grace we have become God's priestly people.

The celebration has already begun. At this table we recall His sacrifice and His love that has saved us from our sins, and that has put a new song in our hearts.

Date Used: _____

Ordination Service

Paul, in his parting speech to the elders from the church in Ephesus, said this: "Take heed to yourselves and to all the flock, in which the Holy Spirit has made you overseers, to care for the church of God which he obtained with the blood of his own Son" (Acts 20:28).

The responsibility of being a leader in the church of God—whether as an elder or deacon, minister of missionary, teacher or other church leader—is a high and holy calling. It does not come about merely by the process of the church's ordaining, but also by the designation and calling of the Holy Spirit.

The church is precious to God because it was purchased and obtained by the shed blood of His only begotten Son, Jesus, and its care and oversight are not to be taken lightly.

Whatever our calling, whatever our gifts, we come to this table now as one body of believers, all servants, all sinners saved by grace. As we eat this bread and drink this cup, we remember that it is by the death of Jesus that we are saved, and by His grace that we are His people.

Date Used: _____

Special Communion Service

Just as the cross is central to the gospel, the Communion is central to the church's worship. The breaking of bread has been an essential part of our worship since the church began. "And they devoted themselves to the apostles' teaching and fellowship, to the breaking of bread and the prayers" (Acts 2:42).

The purpose of this symbolic meal is to remind us that Jesus suffered and died upon the cross as a sacrifice for our sins. Jesus said, "This is my body which is for you. Do this in remembrance of me" (1 Corinthians 11:24b).

Its purpose is also to remind us of the ongoing relationship we have with Christ and the commitment we have made to Him. Jesus also said, "This cup is the new covenant in my blood. Do this, as often as you drink it, in remembrance of me" (1 Corinthians 11:25b).

And its purpose is to remind us of what the Lord has promised is yet to come. As Paul explained it, "For as often as you eat this bread and drink the cup, you proclaim the Lord's death until he comes" (1 Corinthians 11:26).

The dimensions of the Lord's Supper are past, present, and future. The past is the *cross;* the present is the *covenant;* the future is the *coming.*

It is with sincere gratitude and deep humility that we partake of these emblems, giving God the praise and the glory for the gift of His Son Jesus, our Lord and our Savior.

Date Used: _____

Wedding Ceremony

"Therefore a man leaves his father and his mother and cleaves to his wife, and they become one flesh" (Genesis 2:24). This is the deepest, most intimate relationship that a man and a woman may experience, humanly speaking. It is the relationship of marriage.

But there is yet a deeper, spiritual relationship that is possible between two people. It comes when they not only are bound together in marriage, but they are also bound together by their common faith in Jesus Christ.

In marriage you are husband and wife, one flesh. In Christ you are brother and sister, one spirit.

This unity is made possible for you by Christ's death upon the cross. His body was broken and His blood was shed that you might have the forgiveness of your sins, and that you might enjoy the abundant life that only Christ can give, both now and forevermore.

These emblems are to remind you of His body and His blood. They are to remind you that Christ abides in you and you in Him. And they are to remind you of that special unity that you share in Christ and with one another.

Date Used: _____

Preparing and Presenting Communion Meditations

Being a worship leader and presenting the Communion meditation is a task that should not be taken lightly. This is the role of the prophet, the "mouthpiece of God," His spokesman. Your objective is to say what God would have you say and to be what He would have you be.

How well you prepare and present the Communion meditation is very important. The following guidelines will help you think through your role and responsibilities and be ready to give God and His people your very best.

1. *Spend time in prayer.* Prayer is the single most important ingredient in your preparation. Speak to God. Ask Him what He would have you say. Seek His direction, wisdom, and strength for this particular task. Never take for granted or underestimate the power of His partnership, particularly in the assignments you undertake for Him.

2. *Listen to God.* Wait upon the Lord. Spend time in His Word. What you read and discover there will bene-

fit you far greater than anything else you might read or hear. Then, having first listened to God, listen to others. Check the commentaries, read books about the Lord's Supper and sermons on the cross, use resource books such as this one, and listen to the people in your congregation. Keep in touch with God and with others.

3. *Understand your purpose.* What is the purpose of having a Communion meditation in the worship service? What should you hope to accomplish? Don't let this become a routine, empty "time-filler" in the worship service. It is easy for people's minds to wander or shift into neutral or be distracted by other things. Help them to concentrate on what they are doing so that they rightly discern the body of our Lord when they partake. Provide a focus that will enable them to meditate and to commune with the Lord and with one another. Direct their attention to Christ and the cross.

4. *Make your point.* The meanings of the Communion are many faceted. You cannot begin to cover them all, not even the primary meanings, in one meditation. What is your point? What will be the focus of your meditation? Decide on your theme or topic—what you feel God wants you to emphasize or what you believe the congregation most needs—and stick with it throughout your meditation. A single point, well made, will add clarity and power to your presentation.

5. *Plan your meditation.* Perhaps the least desirable way to present a Communion meditation would be just to read one from a book. Plan ahead for an effective, thoughtful presentation that will be understood and appreciated. Make notes when you pray and read and reflect on daily events that may touch on the point you are planning to make. Organize them into an outline or make a list of things you want to include in your pre-

sentation. Write out your meditation if you can. If you are using one from this book, rewrite it in your own words. Adapt it. Add your own illustrations. Make it your own. A little planning goes along way toward accomplishing your purpose and making your point.

6. *Practice out loud.* Whether you are reading or speaking from notes or an outline, practice is important. If your presentation is not orderly and in focus, how can the thoughts and meditations of the worshipers possibly be? In fact, you run the risk of distracting them from worship instead of helping them with it. Your goal is not to produce a perfect, polished performance, but a poorly read or badly presented meditation is inexcusable. Practice.

7. *Time your meditation.* We live in a time-conscious, impatient society. If your meditation lasts longer than your audience's attention span, you will lose them and fail in your purpose. Be sensitive to the time allotted in your service for the Communion meditation as well as to the expectation of the congregation. Three to four minutes should be sufficient. Time your meditation once or twice and make cuts or adjustments if necessary. It will be well worth your effort.

8. *Get your rest.* How you prepare yourself is also directly related to how well you present your meditation. When you stand before your congregation you should be physically refreshed and mentally alert. Avoid late, late minute preparations or other unnecessary activities that might keep you up too late the night before your presentation. Get your rest to do your best.

9. *Look in the mirror.* That may sound vain, but it really isn't. Check your appearance before you stand up in front of people to speak. You do not want to attract attention to yourself. You can do this by overdressing and appearing too "flashy." You can also do

this having a turned up collar, a crooked tie, disheveled hair, or egg on your face! A neat and natural appearance is best. After all, your object is to direct people's attention and thoughts to God, not to yourself.

10. *Take an attitude check.* Self-examination should begin early in the week for the one who is to preside at the Lord's table. Integrity and humility are the key attitudes. Pray for them. Don't plan to say something in your meditation that you do not personally believe and practice. That would be dishonest. Don't try to "put on airs" or be something you are not. Just be yourself, but be your best self.

"So whether you eat or drink, or whatever you do, do all to the glory of God" (1 Corinthians 10:31).

Scripture Resources
for
Communion Meditations

The following themes and Scriptures are relevant for use in Communion meditations. They are offered for your use in developing your own meditations or just for your own personal reading and meditating.

The themes and Scriptures I have used earlier in this book are included here. Many other themes and Scriptures would also be good to use. This list is intended to help you get started; it is by no means exhaustive.

Some of these Scriptures are directly related to the Lord's Supper while others are less obvious in their relation. Some could be read without comment while others require some creative thinking and application. Use your own judgment. If you do not see that a verse is appropriate or useful, select another. I have used the *Revised Standard Version* of the Bible in making the following recommendations.

Acceptance: John 1:9-13; 1 Timothy 1:15, 16

Assurance: John 10:25-30; Acts 17:30, 31; Ephesians

1:11-14; Hebrews 10:19-22; 1 Peter 1:18-21; 1 John 5:12, 13

Atonement: Leviticus 16:23-28; Colossians 1:19-22

Betrayal: Matthew 26:20-25; Mark 14:29, 30, 66-72; Luke 19:41-44; 22:19-22

Blood: Matthew 26:28; John 6:53-55; Romans 5:8, 9; Hebrews 9:13, 14; 1 John 1:6, 7; Revelation 7:13, 14

Body of Christ: Luke 22:19; 1 Corinthians 10:16, 17; 12:12-14

Bread of Life: Luke 24:30, 31; John 6:48-51

Brotherhood: 1 Corinthians 10:16, 17; Hebrews 2:10-13

Christ: Acts 4:12; Hebrews 13:8

Church: Acts 2:1-4; 20:28; Colossians 1:18-20

Comfort: John 14:18, 19; 14:25-27; 2 Corinthians 1:3-7

Commitment: Psalms 37:5, 6; Luke 9:51

Confession: Luke 9:18-22; Romans 10:8-11; 1 John 1:9; 4:13-15

Covenant: Mark 14:22-25; Ephesians 2:11-16; Hebrews 9:15-22

Cross: Matthew 27:32-37; Mark 8:34, 35; 1 Corinthians 1:18, 21-25; Galatians 6:14; Ephesians 2:13-16; Philippians 2:8-11; Hebrews 12:1, 2

Death: Luke 23:44-49; Romans 6:9-11; 2 Timothy 2:11-13; Hebrews 2:14, 15

Discipleship: Isaiah 6:7, 8; Matthew 10:24; Matthew 28:19, 20; Mark 8:34, 35

Doubt: Mark 11:22, 23; Luke 24:36-40; John 20:24-29; Romans 14:23

Faith: John 3:14-16; 19:32-37; Romans 3:21-26; 1 John 4:14-16; 5:4, 5; 5:11-13

Family: Luke 8:19-21; John 19:25-27

Fellowship: 1 John 1:6, 7; Revelation 3:20

Forgiveness: Mark 11:25; Luke 23:32-34; Hebrews 9:22

Freedom from Sin: Psalms 146:5-7; Romans 6:5-7; 6:6-18

Frequency: Acts 2:42, 46; 20:7; 1 Corinthians 11:25

Gratitude: Psalms 50:14, 15; Matthew 15:36; 1 Corinthians 1:3, 4; 11:23, 24; 2 Corinthians 9:10-12; 9:15

Grace: Romans 3:23, 24; 5:17; Ephesians 1:5-8; 2:4-10; Hebrews 2:9

Humility: Luke 9:46-48; Romans 12:3-5; Philippians 2:1-11; James 4:6-10

Joy: Psalms 51:10-12; John 15:11; Hebrews 12:2, 3

Judgment: Matthew 7:1-5; John 12:31-33; 1 Corinthians 11:27-32; Hebrews 4:12, 13; 9:27, 28; 10:29-31; 1 Peter 4:1-5

Love: John 3:16, 17; 15:13; 21:15-17; Romans 5:6-11; 1 John 4:10-12; 4:19-21

Obedience: Romans 5:18, 19; Philippians 2:8; Hebrews 5:8, 9; 1 John 1:5-7

Providence: Psalms 23:5, 6; Isaiah 32:1,2; Matthew 6:31-33; Mark 6:39-44; 2 Corinthians 9:10-15

Purpose: 1 Corinthians 11:23-26

Remembrance: Deuteronomy 8:18, 19; Luke 22:19; 1 Corinthians 11:23-25; Colossians 3:1-4

Repentance: Psalms 51:17; Luke 15:7; Acts 2:36-38; 17:30, 31

Sacrifice: Isaiah 53:4-7; Romans 12:1; 1 Corinthians 5:7; Ephesians 5:1, 2; Hebrews 7:27; 13:12-16; 1 Peter 2:4, 5

Salvation: Psalms 68:19, 20; John 3:16, 17; Philippians 2:12, 13; Hebrews 2:2, 3; 1 Peter 2:1-3

Second Coming: 1 Corinthians 11:26; Hebrews 9:27, 28; Revelation 19:11-16

Self-Examination: Matthew 26:20-22; 1 Corinthians 11:27-29

Sin: Isaiah 53:4-6; Ezekiel 18:4; Romans 6:12-14; 8:1-4; 13:11-14; Hebrews 7:26-28; 1 John 1:8-10; 2:1, 2

Suffering: Matthew 27:27-31; 27:45-50; 2 Corinthians 4:16-18; Hebrews 12:3-5; 1 Peter 2:21-24; 3:14; 4:12-14

Unity: John 15:1-4; 17:20-23; 1 Corinthians 10:16, 17; Ephesians 2:13-16; Revelation 3:20

Witness: Isaiah 6:7, 8; Luke 24:45-49; 1 Corinthians 11:26

Worship: Acts 2:43-47; Revelation 22:1-5